FAMILY BUSINESS

PUNCH
in the Home

Edited by William Hewison

A PUNCH BOOK
Published in association with
GRAFTON BOOKS
A Division of the Collins Publishing Group

Grafton Books
A Division of the Collins Publishing Group
8 Grafton Street, London W1X 3LA

Published by Grafton Books 1988

Copyright © Punch Publications Limited 1988

British Library Cataloguing in Publication Data

Family business: Punch in the home.
1. English humorous cartoons – Collections
I. Hewison, William, *1925* –   II. Punch
741.5'942

ISBN 0-246-13401-1

Printed in Great Britain by William Collins Sons & Co. Ltd, Glasgow

All rights reserved. No part of this publication may be reproduced, stored in a retrieval system, or transmitted, in any form or by any means, electronic, mechanical, photocopying, recording or otherwise, without the prior permission of the publisher.

Introduction

She stands, waiting. A massive figure, her head balanced on a stack of chins, her arms the arms of a top-class weightlifter, her chest billowing out like a spinnaker before the wind, her face knotted into a scowl severe enough to scare a veteran sergeant of the SAS. She's in her dressing-gown, her hair is in curlers, her right hand grasps a rolling-pin. She stands at the bottom of the stairs and watches the front door.

You've seen her more times than you can remember, most often on seaside postcards and in the pop papers, and very occasionally in the pages of *Punch*. She is a cartoon cliché – the gorgon wife awaiting the return of a wayward, tippling husband. In the smarter cartoons there is a clock fixed to the wall with its pointers indicating ten minutes past three, and a window showing a waning moon against a black sky. This, then, is probably the archetypal comment on the matrimonial state.

There's more to it than that, of course, as *Punch* cartoonists are well aware. They have ranged freely over the whole terrain of family life in pursuit of a joke idea, sometimes treading along familiar tracks, sometimes taking a chance in unexplored territory. Family life is real and it is familiar and maybe for that reason a great many of the cartoons dealing with the subject are what is known in the trade as Recognition Humour. The purpose of this category is to latch on to some recognisable facet of everyday life and then push it so that the humour lying just below the surface is prised up into view. This kind of cartoon scores because something we have known as humdrum and ordinary has been re-cast in a comic mould. Starke and Graham, as you will see in this collection, are among the masters of this approach. Because Recognition Humour is principally concerned with human nature and common experience, it has been argued that it is basically superior to the flashy, esoteric stuff which goes under the labels of *zany* and *surreal*. Well, maybe so, maybe not. It is certainly not 'clever-clever'; there are no intellectual barriers to its appreciation.

So what about this wide, familiar terrain? It is not surprising that the cartoonist will devote much of his creative energies to the argy-bargy and conflicts that go on within the perimeter fence of *Dunromin* and *Mon Repos*; apart from that gorgon at the door there is a long line of bickering couples, awkward teenagers, demanding kids – paving the way to that other cliché, the office of the Marriage Counsellor. But that does not mean that our joker ignores the more amiable side of home life, such as competing with the neighbours, keeping up with the latest fads and fashions, battling with home-decorating and the hazards of DIY. Then there's the husband dutifully met at the railway station and the husband who arrives home to one of those 'Your dinner is in the dog' messages. Even nostalgia, in the shape of a rummage among the dusty clobber in the loft, gets a passing glance.

Neither does the cartoonist miss the golf widow and the bridge-party widower, and the layabout, grown-up offspring who won't leave home. And the wives who are going back to Mother and who *do* leave home, suitcases packed, with a husband (this one seen by Starke) 'pleading' for her to stay whilst at the same time he practises his putting on the living-room carpet. This example is very much a man's view of the episode, Leslie Starke being a man. That doesn't mean that women cartoonists, few as they are, can't dish it out appropriately when the situation presents them with a suitable target. Look out for the signatures of Harpur, Duncan, and Sally Artz – I reckon that their pens are a darn sight mightier than any wooden rolling-pin.

William Hewison
March 1988

"She's practising, that's what she's doing."

"The way she kept on about not minding when Willie broke her precious Wedgwood vase!"

"Hello, wall. Did you have a good day today? My big news is I discovered a new, miracle washday product that has me all excited…"

"Arnold's tried everything – LSD, pot, hashish, alcohol – but he always comes back to his old dummy."

"I'm afraid they don't **make** denim nappies, madam."

"See what I mean? No sense of humour."

"Come on, woman – you've only to say 'Sorry we missed you.' They might be back any minute."

"Speaking..."

"If you but knew how much that implement dates you!"

"I think he means it this time."

"We have a perfect marriage. Why spoil it by whining for a divorce?"

"You realise, Deirdre, that sooner or later we'll have to tell her she's adopted."

"Son, have you thought that very soon you'll be old enough to spoil your ballot paper?"

"This one's in marvellous condition. His first wife was a little old lady who hardly used him."

"By the way, do you remember where I put that bottle we were saving for some rather special occasion?"

"Can't you toss a coin or something? One of you has **got** to have custody of him."

"Yes, darling! Mummy has to keep her hands lovely in case she ever wants to go back to brain surgery."

"I worry sometimes that he lacks a man's condescension."

"For heaven's sake, Gerald, must you keep bringing your socialism home with you?"

"Enid, some day you're going to make someone a fine air hostess."

"Next, set the points of the mortise gauge as far apart as the width of the chisel."

"It's nice of you to meet me every night Gladys, but…"

"Mummy! The Bramsons have descended on us."

"Well, he certainly doesn't take after my side."

"I was quite worried for a while."

"What did the psychiatrist say to you, Ma?"

"It's a single-parent family and a social worker."

"Oh, for Pete's sake let him dial it."

"Our trial marriage has been blessed by a trial pregnancy."

"You're supposed to be looking for a camp-bed!"

"That looks great! Now, what do you fancy for your bridesmaids?"

"You'll want your umbrella."

"There won't be any peace now he's seen the ants' eggs."

"The kettle's boiling."

"I'll give you just five seconds to get out of my boots!"

"And don't forget you'll lose your residents' priority parking!"

"How's it going?"

"...and Horace is signalling **his** delight at your dinner invitation."

"Norbert! I hardly recognised you without your morning newspaper!"

"See if you can find a fire-engine – he wants one for his birthday."

"Well, if Teddy refuses to pay alimony to Sindy, you must get a court order."

"I've locked Johnny into the library by way of punishment."

"We're not allowed home before midnight – there's a teenage rave party."

"I've thought of a way to get him to shave the damned thing off — tell him the beard makes him look very distinguished."

"All right — you take the left side, I'll take the right."

"I wish to report a missing person. I understand it is a legal requirement."

"Come and see, Jeremy. The telephone is getting the benefit of one of Daddy's rare smiles."

"I can't stand him, really, but I quite like dressing him up."

"Permission to enter the control room?"

"Getting stoned, being sick and breaking wind is only a part of our alternative culture – there's much more to it than that, Dad."

"This Christmas I'm giving you your own account at a reputable tailor's – and I've already incurred a small debt there just to start you off."

"I'm afraid Mummy has gone to live with a man who has his own extending ladder."

"Yes, I would definitely think that hard-boiled egg has been deserted by its owner."

"Grandpa, tell me again the legend of Judy Garland, queen of Tinsel Town."

"I think he's unwound now…"

"We live on health foods. My husband is a coward."

"Right, that's Stage One of my plan to dominate the world successfully accomplished!"

"It's a type of butterscotch…"

"I'd like to stop off at the newsagent and cancel my copies of 'Bachelor Girl,' 'Bride' and 'Glamour' and order 'Wife', 'Home' and 'Mothercraft'."

"Son, your mother and I had hoped for more badges on your anorak by now."

"The wife's a bit fussy about ash on the carpet…"

"I shouldn't worry. They'll grow out of it."

"You needn't breathe a sigh of relief – I haven't finished yet."

"Since you ask, I had you, Samantha, because the birthrate was falling; and you, David, as revenge on society; and you, Mark, as a bid for lost youth; and you, Jason, were a mistake."

"Guess what? No more sitting up for her, no more Pop, no more teenage rave parties, no more being patronised by bearded boy friends – she's eloped."

"We're absolutely thrilled with his contempt for worldly possessions."

"All right, you win, darling. I'll go along and see these Marriage Guidance people."

"It's what he asked for."

"Shouldn't we get someone in to do that sort of thing, Mother?"

"I often wonder whether it wouldn't be simpler to ransack the house ourselves before we go out."

"It's not his transvestism...it's just that he's giving himself a bigger dress allowance than he's giving me..."

"Shall we carry on with our idyllic existence or shall we break for coffee?"

"I'm popping out for a sex change, dear. If a man comes to the door, make sure it's me before you let him in."

"Your wife rang me to remind you to send me out for her birthday present from you!"

"If you're bored you could always get a part-time job at the power station."

"My! When I last called, your pile of child care magazines was only that high."

"Surely it's long past his bedtime."

"He focused!"

"Before we leave I'll get him to wash the tea cups."

"Nine years old and he doesn't even know how to manipulate his parents."

"And now, he'll put it all together again."

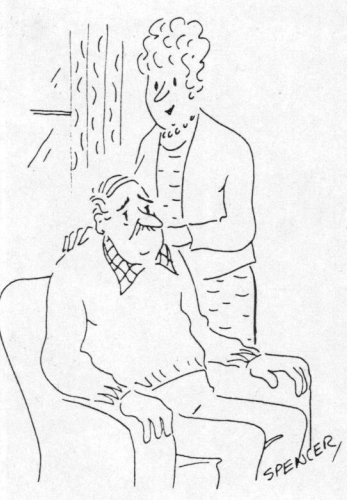

"Look on the bright side, dear – when Mozart was your age he'd been dead fifteen years…"

"You can always tell the ones from large families."

"Did you plan it, or goof it?"

"That's Marcus in his prime – proud, arrogant and top of the heap, yet tenderness itself with his loved ones. I forget who the man is."

"Can you imagine what it will be like in a few years' time — I'll be slopping around the house full of pills, and you'll be wondering where you went wrong, plus the fact that we won't be able to communicate..."

"I get restless in the spring. I wish the council would make us move on."

"Try to get it right this time – I'll smile just once more!"

"It'll be a heavenly place for us to retire to – whenever my wife gets stroppy!"

"Are you stinko or have you come crawling back to me?"

"For heaven's sake! **Pretend** it's an adventure playground."

"You ruin that child."

"I'm not quite sure how to put this, darling, but ever since we've had the house modernised, you don't fit in any more."

"I mean, it's obvious. Replace them by microfilm and the table falls over."

"Put it to your ear and you'll hear the faraway hissing of your father."

"All that small print has given me a headache."

"Well, well! Remember that? My pedestal!"

"Audrey, I've decided **not** to leave you, after all."

"It is I, Franklin, the father figure, home to the
family unit and ready for interaction."

"Once upon a time — well, yesterday, actually…"

"Can't I plead with you, Helen? It isn't my wish that our marriage should end like this."

"Of course, he's only a dog substitute, really."

"I wouldn't worry too much about Jonathan's desire to conform. It's probably just an attention-getting device."

"I hope you're really ill – you know I don't like making house calls, and for goodness sake stop moaning about how seldom I visit you, mother!"

"I'm worried about Tristram — he's still reading adult publications."

"You're out! Off-side!"

"Somebody's Daddy obviously didn't keep up the maintenance payments."

"Trevor went and bought this super table with his own hands, didn't you, Trevor?"

"We have a suspicion there may be a wolf under Mickey's bed."

"Your mother thinks it's time we had a chat about the 'Facts of Life', son."

"Irwin, some young hussy for you on the cordless phone…"

"One of the joys of a family-owned business is that we can enjoy our Sunday dinner while having a Board Meeting at the same time."

"You've never seen one? All right then, we'll play Hunt-the-Sewing-Machine."

"Lack of communication? Don't talk to **me** about lack of communication."

"Son, a man wears his blood group necklace inside his shirt."

"Ruddy marvellous! We agreed to stay together for the sake of the children, and then the little buggers have us both put in the same home!"

"Look, if it upsets you so much, Harry…"

"It's not fair. The rich get richer, the poor get poorer but the comfortably well-off just stay comfortably well-off."

"Why **should** I move over?...I passed!"

"I'll say this much for my Bertha – she's always tried to make marriage exciting…"

"...and here's another one at six months!"

"Lionel likes to spend traditional family evenings around the piano."

"Could you help me for a moment, Henry dear – I'm having a bit of trouble with my zip."

"I notice that when you're talking to yourself you never snarl."

"It worked! We've sent each one home with a gerbil."

"No flowers. That means you want me to think you haven't got a guilty conscience."

"Fascinating detail of big-business pressures and sustained excitement of nightmare journey through fog fail to disguise basic weakness of story line. Not one of this plotsmith's best."

"Previous owners, Protestant family – hardly used!"

"Blow out the candles and make a wish: we've already made ours."

"Is it something I've done? Is it something I've not done? Is it something I've said? Is it something I haven't said, or is it the way I didn't say it?"

"Suddenly, there was an ear-splitting crash as he slammed the filing-cabinet drawer home. 'My God, Hilton!' he hissed, 'You were right all along – it was filed under Miscellaneous!'"

"Of course, quads were quite a shock at first."

"Nancy, if you insist on staying up with the grownups — and of course we're delighted to have you — you must allow us to make an occasional remark that goes over your head."

"Oh, thank God! When I saw the van parked outside, I thought we had big trouble!"

"You and I are very fortunate. There are some children who can't bleep their mother."

"Well, it doesn't seem like a second honeymoon to me."

"Now that the children are grown and gone, you know what I miss? I miss using 'the kids are sick' as an excuse."

"If you'd led a diamond they'd have been four down!"

"I'm determined to have the baby the way nature intended. I've booked into a natural childbirth clinic in Geneva."

"For heaven's sake, Mary! Can't you see I'm in conference!"

"Of course, Margaret working is a great help. She buys all her own gin."

"One by one, they all grew up…left home…married…divorced…came drifting back…"

"Not my stick insect!"

"We feel we've made a real breakthrough with the kid's room."